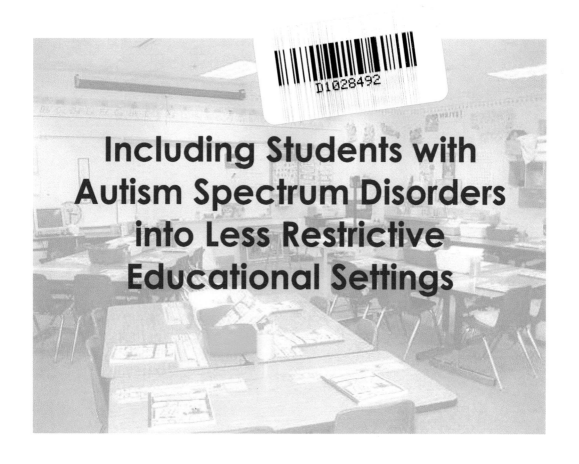

Including Students with Autism Spectrum Disorders into Less Restrictive Educational Settings

Edited By:

Joanne Gerenser, Ph.D., CCC-SLP
Mary E. McDonald, Ph.D., BCBA-D

"Great teachers empathize with kids, respect them, and believe that each one has something special that can be built upon."

~Ann Lieberman

Acknowledgements

We would like to extend our gratitude to the following staff at the Eden II/Genesis Programs who supported, proofread, and contributed to the chapters within this document. In addition, thanks to those individuals who are the inspiration and impetus for this work – the parents and children with whom we have the privilege and honor of working and who have taught us so much.

Dana Battaglia, M.Phil., CCC-SLP
Frank Cicero, Ph.D., BCBA
Catherine Falleo, MS Ed., SAS, SDA
Catherine Hamilton, LMSW, BCBA
Randy Horowitz, MS Ed., SAS
Cynthia Lloyd, MBA, SDA
Nancy Phillips, BA
Joanne Sgambati, Ph.D., BCBA
Erin Sparacio, MS Ed., SAS, SDA
Irene Stefa, MA
Joyann Tramuta

ISBN-10 1452849412
EAN-13 9781452849416

TABLE OF CONTENTS

NOTES:

1. INTRODUCTION

Goals of Inclusion

Implementing instructional programs for students with autism can be challenging. This challenge is highlighted by the fact that no two students with autism are alike and each requires individualized programming. The decision to initiate specific goals and objectives relating to inclusion must be made systematically and responsibly, with input from the student's parents and members of the educational team.

There are many important components to include when developing individualized inclusion goals. One is a careful identification of the skills and behaviors the student needs to acquire in order to benefit from the inclusion placement. Another is a clear understanding of the student's strengths and weaknesses in order to address them programmatically and systematically.

A comprehensive inclusion curriculum for students with autism consists of goals and objectives that can be categorized in two ways:

1. Maintenance and generalization of skills and behaviors that have been acquired in more structured settings; and

2. Acquisition of new skills and behaviors in the inclusion site.

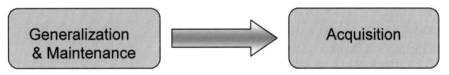

Initially, the focus of inclusion is on the generalization of skills and maintenance of appropriate behavior. Once the student begins practicing skills and behaviors that have been learned through more structured teaching in relatively smaller groups, the focus should shift *from* generalization of skills *to* the acquisition of new skills in the inclusive environment.

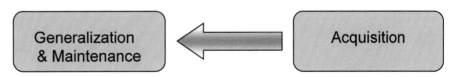

A preliminary listing of goals that would be important for students practice in the inclusive environment may include:

1. Following group instructions.

2. Attending during group instruction for a sustained period.

3. Imitating peers' appropriate behavior.

4. Exhibiting observational learning skills.

5. Discriminating between when to imitate peers and when to do one's own work.

6. Responding to and initiating communication with peers.

7. Transitioning between activities.

8. Engaging in appropriate play/recreation skills.

9. Remaining on task during independent work activities.

10. Making appropriate use of free time.

11. Asking for assistance when needed.

12. Discriminating between when to raise one's hand and when it is not appropriate.

13. Developing appropriate social skills (i.e. friendship).

14. Developing coping skills (i.e. learning how to handle frustration, anger, anxiety).

15. Responding to delayed contingencies.

16. Responding to group contingencies.

17. Learning to self-monitor behavior.

IDEA, IDEIA and LRE

Individuals with Disabilities Education Act (IDEA) This federal legislation requires that each state establish procedures to assure that students with disabilities are educated to the maximum extent appropriate with students without disabilities (Osborne & Di Mattia, 1994). IDEA mandates that districts consider inclusion options for students with disabilities.

IDEIA 2004 The new Individuals with Disabilities Education Improvement Act (IDEIA) 2004 regulations contain changes in several important areas, including revised methods to identify students with learning disabilities, early intervening services, highly qualified teachers, discipline, and meeting accessibility standards.

IDEIA has 6 main tenets:

1. Zero reject- Schools are responsible for the education of *all* children, regardless of the degree of disability.

2. Least restrictive environment- Students with disabilities should be educated with typical students to the maximum extent appropriate with any needed supports.

3. Non-discriminatory assessment-Assessment must be non-biased.

4. Free and appropriate public education (FAPE) - Students must be provided an appropriate education developed in an Individualized Education Program (IEP) at public expense.

5. Due process- School must protect the rights of students and their parents.

6. Parent and Student Participation- School must share decision making on educational services with the student and the parents.

No Child Left Behind Act (NCLB) is federal legislation that seeks to improve the performance of Unites States schools by requiring that each state to establish assessments of academic skills in certain grades in order to receive federal funding. *"No Child Left Behind"* is based on stronger accountability for results, more freedom for states and communities, proven education methods, and more choices for parents." (http://www2.ed.gov/nclb/overview/intro/4pillars.html).

Response to Intervention (RtI) RtI is a type of academic intervention that uses a 3- tiered process to provide support at systematically increasing levels as needed for students who are in need of such supports. Specifically, RTI involves the use of evidence-based interventions and progress monitoring.

The Family Education Rights and Privacy Act (FERPA) The Family Educational Rights and Privacy Act (FERPA) (20 U.S.C. § 1232g; 34 CFR Part 99) is a Federal law that protects the privacy of student education records. The law applies to all schools that receive funds under an applicable program of the U.S. Department of Education

Least Restrictive Environment (LRE) The Least Restrictive Environment stipulates that students with disabilities may be placed into special classes, separate schools, or other removal from the regular educational environment *only* when the nature or severity of the student's disability is such that, even with the use of supplementary aids and services, learning cannot be satisfactorily achieved. The placement of an individual student with a disability in the least restrictive environment shall:

1. Provide the special education services needed by the student;

2. Provide for the special education of the student to the maximum extent appropriate with other students who do not have disabilities; and

3. Be as close as possible to the student's home.

"The Least Restrictive Environment" is the legally controlling term under federal law to determine the proper placement for a student with disabilities. The terms "full inclusion" and "mainstreaming" are widely used, but least restrictive environment is the legal standard for providing a Free Appropriate Public Education (FAPE), also guaranteed by federal law.

An example of Application of LRE for a student with autism:

If providing a student with autism with needed supports (e.g., modifications, a 1:1 aide, related services) allows the general education classroom to remain an appropriate placement for the student- this would then be considered the Least Restrictive Environment. Therefore a student should be provided with any and all supports that would allow him/her to remain in the general education classroom if this is appropriate for the student. It would be less restrictive for a student to be assigned a 1:1 aide to shadow the student in the general education class than to place the student in a self-contained classroom.

2. DEFINITIONS AND TERMS

ACCOMMODATIONS are the provisions made to allow a student to access and demonstrate learning. Accommodations do not substantially change the instructional level, the content or the performance criteria. Rather, accommodations are made in order to provide a student equal access to learning and equal opportunity to demonstrate what is known. Accommodations do not alter the content of the test or provide inappropriate assistance to the student within the context of the test. Examples of accommodations may include books on tape, content enhancements, and allowing additional time to take a test.

ADAPTATION involves an adjustment of the instructional content or performance expectations of students with disabilities from what is expected or taught to students in general education. Adaptations are usually included as part of a student's Individualized Educational Program (IEP). Examples of adaptations can include decreasing the number of exercises the student is expected to complete, assignment of different reading materials, or use of a calculator instead of working out problems by hand.

APPLIED BEHAVIOR ANALYSIS (ABA) systematically applies procedures derived from the principles of behavior to improve socially significant behavior, and to demonstrate experimentally that the procedures employed were responsible for the improvement in behavior (Cooper, Heron, & Heward, 2007). ABA emphasizes the use of specific instructional techniques to change behavior in systematic and measurable ways.

AUTISM/ BEHAVIORAL CONSULTANT is a person who provides *recommendations to the staff* at an inclusion site to enhance the inclusion experiences of a student with autism. These recommendations are derived from observation, interviews with relevant staff, and analysis of data. Consultation differs from supervision in that the recommendations are given as suggestions rather than mandates.

EXTENDED SCHOOL DAY refers to a provision for a special education student to receive instruction for a period longer than the standard school day. This may include later afternoons or earlier starting times. This may include receiving education for twelve months rather than 10.

EXTENDED SCHOOL YEAR refers to a provision for a special education student to receive instruction during ordinary school "vacation" periods.

FULL INCLUSION describes a program in which a student with autism or pervasive developmental disorder (PDD) is placed *full time* in a general education program. The student may or may not be accompanied by a shadow, who provides assistance to help the student benefit from the inclusion placement. All areas of education and the fulfillment of all IEP mandates, with the possible exception of related services, are met in the mainstream setting.

FUNCTIONAL COMMUNICATION TRAINING (FCT): is defined as a proactive approach to reduce maladaptive behaviors (Carr & Durand, 1985; Durand, 1999). FCT involves two major components; (1) Identifying the function of a behavior, and (2) teaching an appropriate communication skill to serve the same function as the behavior under observation.

FUNCTIONAL CURRICULUM is defined as a curriculum focused on practical life skills and usually taught in community based settings with concrete materials that are a regular part of everyday life. The purpose of this type of instruction is to maximize the student's generalization to real life use if his/her skills.

IEP- INDIVIDUALIZED EDUCATION PROGRAM is the document developed at an IEP meeting which sets the standard by which subsequent special education services are usually determined appropriate. It is a legally binding document.

INCLUSION is defined as the provision of services to students with disabilities, including those with severe impairments, in the neighborhood school, in age-appropriate general education classes. This provision of services should be implemented with the necessary support services and supplementary aids (for the student and teacher) both to assure the student's success (academically, behaviorally, and socially) and to prepare the student to participate as a full and contributing member of the society (Lipsky & Gartner, 1996).

MAINSTREAMING refers to the *limited and selective placement* of students with special needs *into one or more general education classes or activities* such as recess or lunch.

MODIFICATIONS are changes to what the student is expected to learn. They are provided to students with disabilities who are working below grade level and who may require modified expectations within a given activity to meet their individual needs. Alternative curriculum goals can be used to make the content more relevant and functional to the student's individual needs. Requirements for a student may be partially adapted, with the student expected to master some, but not all of the expectations. The level of mastery that is expected for a student may be altered.

PERSON-CENTERED PLANNING is a process whereby persons with disabilities, with the support of families, direct the planning and allocation of resources to meet their own life vision and goals. This planning process is based on a person's preferences, aspirations and needs; understands how a person makes decisions; understands how a person is and can be productive; discovers what the person loves and dislikes; encourages and supports long-term hopes and dreams; is supported by a short-term support plan that is based on reasonable costs given the person's support needs; includes the individual's responsibilities; includes a range of supports including funded, community and natural supports; and should be conducted based upon the needs of the individual, but at least annually.

REGRESSION/RECOUPMENT is defined as the amount of loss of skills a child experiences over an instructional break (primarily summer vacation) and the amount of time it takes him/her to recover the lost skills.

RELATED SERVICES means transportation and such developmental, corrective, and other supportive services as are required to assist a child with a disability to benefit from special education, and includes speech-language pathology and audiology services, interpreting services, psychological services, physical and occupational therapy, recreation (including therapeutic recreation), early identification and assessment of disabilities in children, counseling services (including rehabilitation counseling), orientation and mobility services, and medical services for diagnostic or evaluation purposes. Related services also include school health services and school nurse services, social work services in school, and parent counseling and training.

SELF-DETERMINATION refers to individuals making the choices that allow them to exercise control over their own lives, to achieve the goals to which they aspire and to acquire the skills and resources necessary to participate fully and meaningfully in society. The right to self-determination must include individuals with all types of disabilities. Self-Determination has five basic rights and responsibilities: Freedom, Authority, Support, Responsibility and Confirmation.

SHADOW defines the staff person (also called a one to one shadow) *assigned to the student with autism in the inclusion setting.* This staff person is responsible for prompting, promoting successful transitions, facilitating social interactions, delivering reinforcement, preventing and redirecting challenging behavior, and implementing all components of the student's formal behavior plan.

SUPPLEMENTARY AIDES AND SERVICES are provided in order for an eligible individual to be served in the general education classroom, which may include intensive short-term specially designed instruction; educational interpreters; readers for individuals with visual impairments; special education assistant; special education assistants for individuals with physical disabilities for assistants in and about school, and for transportation; materials; and specialized or modified instructionally related equipment for use in the school.

SUPPORT SERVICES are defined as specially designed instruction and activities which augment, supplement, or support the educational program of eligible individuals.

SUPPORTED INCLUSION is defined as full or part time placement of a student with autism or PDD into a regular education program with *some degree of assistance provided* either by a shadow or instructor who accompanies the student, or through access to a special education teacher who previews or overviews teaching material presented in the classroom.

TRANSITION SERVICES are a coordinated set of activities for a child with a disability that (1) is designed to be within the results-oriented process, that is focused on improving the academic and functional achievement of the child with a disability to facilitate the child's movement from school to post-school activities, including post-secondary education, vocational training, integrated employment (including supported employment), continuing and adult education, adult services, independent living, or community participation; (2) is based on the individual child's needs, taking into account the child's strengths, preferences and interests; and (3) includes instruction, related services, community experiences, the development of employment and other post-school adult living objectives, and, when appropriate, acquisition of daily living skills and functional vocational evaluation.

3. DEVELOPING READINESS SKILLS

When beginning an experience in an inclusive setting, it may benefit the student with autism if he/she has some specific readiness skills within his/her repertoire. Skills in the areas of attending, group academic skills, play, socialization and the ability to maintain appropriate behavior are initially taught while the student is in a highly- structured program. Simulated inclusion experiences can then be provided to allow the student to practice and begin to generalize skills previously mastered. The skills needed for each student and for each inclusion experience are different; therefore they must be individualized and tailored to fit the proposed setting. Consider that this does not mean that the student must actually have all of the skills that are discussed in this section. Rather, the more of these skills that a student has, the more successful he/she may be in the inclusion setting.

In the area of **attending**, the essential skills are eye gaze toward materials, sustained attention, joint attention, and the ability to remain in one's seat and on task for specified amounts of time. The student should be taught to attend to necessary materials during task completion. The student must also be taught to remain on task and focused for a sustained period of time, whether sitting or standing at a table, on line, in front of or away from a teacher. Finally, the student must also be taught to respond to his/her name whether in either a quiet setting or one that is noisy and stimulating.

Regarding **group academics**, when entering a program that uses Applied Behavior Analysis (ABA), a student is typically instructed in a one to one, student to teacher ratio. The most important inclusion skills learned this way are imitating and gaining information from the environment, remaining in one's seat and on task for longer periods of time, and responding to delayed contingencies. When these are mastered, the student can begin learning through observation in a dyad (two to one) to remain on task, and to behave and sit appropriately while the teacher is engaged with another student. The student should also learn to return to work without the teacher's direct intervention. Subsequently, group instruction can begin in a larger group setting, such as in a group of three or four. Group responding, as well as hand-raising, are also important readiness skills. A student should also be able to advocate for themselves in a classroom setting to facilitate their own knowledge acquisition. Asking for a teacher's assistance to clarify the nature of an assignment if it is unclear to them is also a critical skill to be developed. Again, this skill can be practiced while in a highly structured, self-contained program, and then practiced and generalized to the inclusion setting. For young students, small group instruction might involve circle time activities like singing, calendar, art, and attending to a story. For an early elementary school student, activities might include an academic group or a leisure activity such as gym.

Group play and socialization are other important skill areas in inclusion. Learning to play, share and socialize are primary activities for preschool students. For older students, socialization occurs primarily during lunch and recess and between classes or lessons. Students in a general education environment need basic social skills in order to be accepted. These include initiating greetings, responding to a peer and obtaining a peer's attention. The student also needs to be taught age-appropriate play skills. For younger students this might involve use of blocks, cars, and puzzles. Pretend play is also an important area of focus. Appropriate play skills for older students include simple board games, team sports, individual leisure activities such as using an aerobics tape, and basic conversational skills appropriate to recess activities (e.g. video games). Teaching play and socialization skills should begin within a highly structured program. It may be difficult to fully expand these skills if the student does not have access to socially appropriate peers, but once in the general education environment, the student can interact with peers so that the play and socialization skills previously taught can be generalized. For older students with adequate literacy skills, written scripts can be used and systematically faded to provide students with the appropriate language for a particular social situation. For students who cannot read, auditory scripts may be useful options.

Challenging or disruptive behavior is another factor that greatly impacts inclusion. The student must be able to respond to the rules and behavioral expectations of inclusive settings and to respond to a system of delayed reinforcement. Prior to inclusion, the student is taught using a token board or behavior contract, systematically increasing the amount of time or tokens needed for reinforcement. Maladaptive behaviors such as hand flapping, inappropriate verbalizations, aggression and self-injurious behaviors must be minimal so the student is not disruptive or stigmatized in the inclusion setting. A formal or informal behavior plan of action may be needed to address maladaptive behaviors. Staff assigned to the student in inclusion should be able to manage the student's behavior prior to working with the student in inclusion.

4. TRANSITION TO LRE

Federal law mandates that all students in restrictive settings have the right to be educated in a less restrictive setting if this is appropriate for the student. In these instances, school districts are required to determine what the least restrictive setting would be for that student. For example, transition to least restrictive environment may mean educating a student with a disability in a general education classroom utilizing supplementary aids and supports.

An individualized assessment may assist the team in making decisions about the environment that would be least restrictive and appropriate for the student. In addition, direct observation with formal data collection is also a helpful piece of information and allows for decision making to be based on data and to be systematic and goal directed. It is important to determine if a student's skills can be further developed in a less restrictive setting at this time. This determination of readiness is based on an evaluation of each student's mastery of skills.

A tool such as the *Inclusion Readiness Checklist* (see Appendix) may help the team to determine areas of strength as well as identify areas in need further attention. The staff at highly structured, self-contained programs initiate a systematic transition through the following process:

1. The student's teacher completes an *Inclusion Readiness Checklist* for each student, evaluating the current level of the skills that will make the inclusion experience more successful.

2. The teacher schedules a meeting with his/her direct supervisor to review the outcomes of the *Inclusion Readiness Checklist* and student's progress toward meeting relevant goals.

3. The student may be given additional testing (e.g., speech, psycho-educational, etc) to further determine the student's needs and abilities. This testing may be followed by a formal recommendation by the clinical team to pursue a less restrictive environment and look for appropriate programs.

4. The supervisor and teacher then typically meet with the parent(s) to discuss the student's readiness to begin the transition to the less restrictive environment. Parents are encouraged to assist in the transition process through meetings, visits to potential educational settings, and CSE meetings.

5. Goals for inclusion are developed at this time with the clinical team and the parents.

6. A transition plan is developed to ensure a successful transition to the Least Restrictive Environment (LRE). (See sample transition plan in Appendix).

Educational Options

Schools

The options available for inclusion settings will depend on the types of programs offered by the child's home school district. The majority of school districts offer the following the continuum of services:

1. Full time general education class (on age/grade level).

2. Full time general education class (below age/grade level). This is appropriate when the student is otherwise well matched to younger typical peers or those who are functioning below grade level.

3. Part time general education and part time
   Special education class, or
   Resource room, or
   Special education class in a separate location

4. Part time special education class and part time
   Resource room, or
   Special education class in a separate location.

5. Full time special education class within an inclusive setting with opportunities for inclusion
   with typical peers.

If the student's home district lacks an appropriate placement for the student, other options to consider may include placement in another school district, private-school placement, or placement in a state-approved private school for students with disabilities who can communicate with and socialize with the student with autism. Non-educational settings can also be considered for after-school and weekend inclusion experiences. Several of these options are listed at the end of this section.

Placement Selection Criteria provide the framework for evaluating potential inclusion sites. Evaluative questions in the domains of program structure, program environment, staffing ration, classroom management, motivational system, and potential staffing at the inclusion site, follow.

General Program structure:

1. What is the age range of the participating students?

2. Is there a classroom schedule or routine? If so, what is the schedule or routine?

3. What are the expectations with regard to adherence to classroom schedule?

4. How consistent is the schedule? What kinds of changes occur to alter the schedule?

5. What skills are necessary to be successful in the program?

Program environment:

1. Where are the important physical and personnel resources in the program, such as bathrooms, exits, entrances, quiet area, and school nurse?

2. Are there distractions in the environment? What are they?

3. What are the seating arrangements in classroom, such as proximity to blackboard, teacher, and peers?

Staffing ratio:

1. What is the group size? Does this change over the course of the day?

2. What is the student : adult ratio?

3. How are one to one shadows used? Are they assigned to a specific student? Do they serve as second teachers in the classroom?

Classroom management:

1. What are the classroom rules? How are the students socialized to them?

2. How does the teacher handle student disruptions and undesired behaviors?

3. How does the teacher reinforce students for desired behavior?

4. How do current students behave during unstructured time?

5. Does the staff have experience implementing formal behavior plans? If so, what type?

Speech, Language, and Communication Management:

1. Are there multiple models of service delivery for speech, language, and communication intervention (e.g. direct service, indirect service, classroom consultation, etc)?

2. Are staff supportive of and adequately trained in the use of various augmentative and alternative communication (AAC) systems as a learning and communication aide for students who require them?

3. Is social skills training incorporated in to the school day? Will student be provided with opportunities to practice these skills with peers?

4. Are there appropriate opportunities for socializing with typical peers?

Motivational systems:

1. Is there a group motivational system in place?

2. Are there individual student motivational systems in place?

Staff Disposition at the inclusion site:

1. How willing is the current staff to cooperate with the proposed inclusion?

2. Does staff see inclusive placements as a burden, a challenge or an opportunity?

3. What types of resources and support systems are available to the staff? How are they used?

4. Are staff able to implement IEP and curriculum adaptations to support student within inclusive settings?

5. Is data collected to demonstrate student progress regarding IEP goals and objectives?

Parent Preparation for Inclusion generally requires:

1. Clarification on personnel role and responsibility for efficient communication and collaboration.

2. Introduction to their new role as team member.

3. Coaching on ways to advocate for their child without being perceived as aggressive by the receiving school.

4. Provision of information by parent about the child.

5. Assistance by parent to promote collaboration across home and school settings.

Portfolio preparation for staff at inclusion site. A portfolio may be created to provide important information prior to the student starting and will be a part of the transition process.

Portfolio may include any and all of the following:

1. Information from child's parents, including details about child's likes and dislikes and any other information parents would like to share about their child (e.g., successes, etc). This may take place in the form of a letter from the parents to the new staff.

2. Teacher (if appropriate) includes information about academics, socialization and behavior, as well as student's current levels and needs.

Sample work could be included in the portfolio to assist the new teacher.

3. Consultant may also wish to include details regarding student's history and future plans.

4. Student may want to include information and or sample work for the new staff.

E. CSE Negotiations to Formalize Placement involve resolution between parent, CSE and student's original placement of the following items prior to inclusion:

1. Development of a Transition Plan for preparation of students, staff, and family.

2. Development of a schedule for the student's day/week

3. Provision of a one to one shadow and clarification regarding who employs, supervises, and covers their absence.

4. Transportation.

5. Provision of consultation, staff training and supervision.

6. Determination of curricular content and clarification of responsibility for teaching academics, activities of daily living (ADL), vocational programs and skills, related services as well as inclusion goals.

7. Determination of specific supplementary aids and supports needed to facilitate student's placement in LRE (e.g., provision of note takers, Augmentative and Alternative Communication (AAC) systems).

8. Determination of criteria for increasing time spent in the inclusion program.

9. Provision for data collection and analysis.

10. A schedule of team meeting time.

11. Determination of the appropriateness of extended school year services, whether and where a summer program is mandated.

Discussion with Inclusion Site Personnel should lead to the following outcomes:

1. Identification of the specific class for inclusion.

2. Identification of specific classroom staff and 1:1 staff if appropriate.

3. A schedule of training in methods of educating students with autism in less restrictive settings.

4. Determination of how to orient peers to the inclusion student. This requires parental cooperation and consent.

5. A protocol for correspondence which identifies contact persons in both settings and parameters for parental involvement and correspondence.

Settings Other than Schools. Based on the nature of the inclusion goals that were developed, other community settings might be suitable. These include but are not limited to:

After-school programs
Play groups
Camps
Participation in team sports
JCC, YMCA, scouts
Vocational placement in the community
Recreational programs, swimming classes
Library programs
Computer and art courses

A commitment to inclusion involves.....

5. ROLES AND RESPONSIBILITIES

All members of the team should have both initial and ongoing orientation and training in order to insure the student's successful transition. Team members must clearly understand not only their own roles but also how they coordinate and interact with those of others. A summary of team member roles follows.

ROLE OF THE TEACHER IN THE INCLUSION SITE

1. Provides a structured classroom with rules and routines.

2. Establishes and individualizes a motivational system to encourage adaptive behavior.

3. Maintains adequate communication with staff in order to establish roles, promotes consistency, and addresses issues in a timely manner.

4. Maintains a low tolerance for inappropriate behavior of students.

5. Fosters a team approach among parents and professionals.

6. Encourages new ideas and feedback from others.

7. Attends team meetings to discuss placement and classroom issues.

8. Recognizes patterns of difficulty and communicates them to the team.

9. Treats the student as a full member of the classroom in order to maximize the student's participation in classroom activities.

10. Provides input to the shadow regarding prompting.

11. Dialogs with parents to determine frequency and nature of communication desired/required; Maintains adequate on-going communication with parents.

12. Modifies curriculum as needed to tailor it to the student's current levels of ability.

13. Implements the goals of the Individualized Educational Plan (IEP).

14. Reports on progress of IEP goals.

ROLE OF THE ONE TO ONE SHADOW

1. Engages students in interactive situations through prompting and fading prompts.

2. Implements individualized motivation systems for the student.

3. Provides direct instruction to the student which previews or reviews classroom learning as needed.

4. Consistently assesses and reassess those activities for which the student is independent and those for which the student requires assistance.

5. Increases own knowledge and understanding of the principles of ABA and the inclusion process.

6. Remains open to new ideas and feedback from others.

7. Works as a team member to enhance student success.

8. Collects objective data regarding behavior.

9. Collects objective data regarding skill acquisition.

10. Adapts easily to classroom activities and includes the student in activities.

11. Assists in training others to interact with and teach the student.

12. Takes direction from the classroom teacher.

13. Assists in making data based decisions concerning integration and fading.

14. Consistently promotes independence by fading themselves back from a task wherever possible.

ROLE OF THE AUTISM/BEHAVIOR CONSULTANT

1. Develops individualized goals to enhance skill acquisition.

2. Task analyzes goals to ensure maximum performance. Assists family and school with curriculum areas needing modification or practice.

3. Creates proactive behavior plans to prevent maladaptive behaviors from occurring in the inclusion setting.

4. Creates formal behavior plans to target and decrease maladaptive behaviors in the inclusion setting.

5. Provides ongoing training and support to school personnel and the shadow.

6. Implements data systems and assists with ongoing data collection and analysis.

7. Possesses and communicates expertise in areas of inclusion, ABA and autism.

8. Participates in team meetings and encourages adequate communication among members of the team.

9. Identifies and provides practice in areas that may be difficult for the student in the inclusion setting.

10. Provides feedback and direction to the shadow.

11. Assists staff in responding to and managing parental concerns and in promoting a collaborative
relationship between home and school.

ROLE OF PARENT AND OTHER HOME-BASED INTERVENTIONISTS

1. Maintains contact with inclusion school personnel through phone contacts, school visits
   and a correspondence notebook as planned.

2. Communicates with the teacher and shadow about events and changes that have occurred or may occur which might affect student's behavior in school, as well as any changes in behavior or new skills learned at home.

3. Shares information with the school team regarding the student's strengths and needs before placement begins.

4. Educates the school team about the student's interests and preferences, and successful behavioral tips.

5. Remains aware of school goals and methods to promote generalization.

6. Is consistent with behavioral issues at home.

7. Learns about popular peer interests and encourages these in the student in order to facilitate socialization.

8. Encourages school personnel to visit the home program, if appropriate.

9. Practices activities at home which might be difficult for the student when attending the inclusion setting.

10. Plans for the generalizing of skills learned at school to the home and other natural environments.

11. Uses creativity to encourage the student to practice inclusion-related skills.

ROLE OF THE COMMITTEE ON SPECIAL EDUCATION
(CSE)

1.   Develops a Transition Plan with flexible timelines.

2.   Develops an IEP which includes specific measurable inclusion goals, objectively written, to ensure success in the inclusion environment.

3.   Encourages revision of the IEP as needed through collection and review of data.

4.   Recommends a one to one shadow on the IEP (as appropriate)

5.   Provides for staff training (initial and ongoing).

6.   Provides for consultation on a specified schedule (e.g., weekly, monthly).

7.   Provides for planning time and clinical team meeting time.

8.   Is accessible to the school-based team.

NOTES:

6. CONSULTATION AND TRAINING OF INCLUSION STAFF

The consultant must tailor training to the needs of the student while taking into account the knowledge and experience of the staff and administration in the inclusion site. A combination of lecture, hands-on training, and modeling of intervention strategies is recommended, along with the ongoing provision of information to further the understanding of the disorder and how it affects this particular student.

The consultant must continually assess the student and his/her team members to acknowledge progress, identify deficits, build necessary skills and modify the school schedule to enable the student to succeed in the program. Outlined below is a hypothetical scenario that suggests specific topics and methods for training each member of this team.

A.   Step 1 - Lecture/Training

These trainings can be provided to school district personnel during the summer or in the school district. Due to the limited funding generally available in districts for training, the depth and breadth of training of team members can be varied. The chart below reflects the most important training needed for each team member. This reflects a minimum level of training to be provided.

Staff Trained	Overview of Autism	Supporting Students in Inclusive Environments	Overview of ABA	Proactive Behavior Management	Reinforce-ment and Prompting	Guidelines for Shadowing
Special Ed Teacher	✓	✓	✓	✓	✓	✓
General Ed Teacher	✓	✓	✓	✓	✓	✓
School Psychologist	✓	✓	✓	✓		
Principal, VP, PPS	✓					
Director or Sup. Of Spec. Ed	✓					
1:1 Shadow	✓	✓	✓	✓	✓	✓

B. Step 2 - Hands On Training:

The consultant explains, models, and shares knowledge of ABA techniques and methodology with the inclusion staff using the methodology enumerated below.

Training Provided by the Consultant to the Inclusion Teacher:

1. Observes the teacher and his/her interactions with the student. Makes recommendations as appropriate.

2. Helps identify prompts and cues that maximize student performance without stigmatizing the student.

3. Discusses the importance of giving simplified directions.

4. Observes classroom management and routines and suggests accommodations or modifications as needed.

5. Reviews the roles of other team members and their interface with those of the teacher.

6. Establishes systems of communication which can be continued by the teacher, such as a home-school communication log, weekly meetings with the one to one shadow and regular team meetings.

Training Provided by the Consultant to the One to One Shadow

1. Observes the one to one shadow and his/her interactions with the student. Makes recommendations as appropriate

2. Models ABA techniques and methodology, focusing on shadowing techniques in a wide range of situations, such as during independent and group work, transition and recess.

3. Models prompting techniques and prompt fading strategies that increase the student's skill acquisition and independence.

4. Models reinforcement techniques, proactive behavior management and redirection strategies that increase or decrease behavior.

5. Discusses the role of data collection, reviews forms and models

procedures.

6. Discusses how and when reinforcement will be lessened (faded), based on student progress.

C. Stage 3 - Ongoing Training

Training Provided by the Consultant to the Inclusion Teacher

1. Observes the teacher and his/her interactions with student.

2. Ensures that the teacher is providing prompts and cues that are not stigmatizing to the student.

3. Explains inclusion techniques and their functions when appropriate.

4. Trains the teacher to provide constructive feedback to the shadow.

5. Assists the teacher in modifying the curriculum to a level appropriate to the student's needs.

6. Provides written feedback

Training Provided by the Consultant to the One to One Shadow

1. Observes the shadow and his/her interactions with the student. Recommends changes as necessary.

2. Models and explains ABA techniques and methodology, focusing on shadowing techniques.

3. Models prompting techniques that increase student independence without stigmatizing the student.

4. Reviews data and data collection to ensure that recording is accurate and appropriate.

5. Provides written feedback.

D. Other Consultant Responsibilities in the Inclusion Setting:

1. Participates in regular team meetings.

2. Coordinates home and school programs when mandated.

3. Facilitates communication between school and family (e.g., develops a home-school correspondence system).

4. Develops behavior management plans when necessary.

5. Devises (creates) data collection systems and trains staff in their implementation.

6. Assists in the development of IEP goals and objectives.

7. Observes potential placement options for the following school year.

8. Provides written feedback and recommendations after each consultation.

9. Participates in CSE meetings.

10. Evaluates the performance of the one to one shadow.

11. Follows school protocol to inform necessary team members about issues relating to the student.

12. Ensures that communication systems are effective and efficient across team members.

13. Identifies maladaptive patterns in student behavior and performance, and implements proactive strategies that enable the student to replace them.

Two examples of self monitoring of behavior follow:

1. The consultant may set up a self-monitoring system for the shadow that will foster independence in the absence of the consultant. The shadow may have a chart that requires him/her to check off once per every twenty minutes that s/he made sure that the student had all necessary materials such as scripts, planner and social story available.

2. The shadow may be asked to collect data on their physical proximity to the student to assist in the shadow fading in and out appropriately as needed.

NOTES:

7. METHODOLOGY

All behavioral methods used by highly structured programs with strong foundations in Applied Behavior Analysis (ABA) both in the self-contained classes and in inclusion settings, are based on empirical research findings. Decisions on modifying the inclusion experience should be based on objective data analysis, direct observation and team discussion.

A. Prompting Strategies: Prompting strategies are used in order to guide a student toward the desired behavior, for instance correct completion of a task or appropriate transition. The nature of the prompt used depends on the level of intrusiveness required to ensure the response, as well as the appropriateness of the prompt in the particular setting. Within inclusion settings in particular, it is of utmost importance that the least restrictive prompt be used so as not to intrude on the inclusion environment. In fact, a student who has been assessed to be able to participate in an inclusion setting should have a large number of prerequisite skills that make the need for intrusive prompts infrequent. Instructional prompts in inclusion settings usually take the form of gestural, verbal, intra-stimulus or written prompts. Low level physical prompts, such as a tap on the shoulder, may be used when necessary and appropriate. All prompts should be faded as soon as the student no longer needs them. If a student continues to require a higher level of prompting than that needed by classmates, the appropriateness of the inclusion setting for that student should be re-evaluated.

B. Reinforcement: Even in inclusion settings, students continue to benefit from the systematic and strategic use of reinforcement procedures. Differential reinforcement is one of the key procedures used to promote adaptive behavior. Reinforcement for appropriate behavior and instructional responding continues to be required in inclusion settings. Both primary and secondary reinforcers may be used. Primary reinforcers such as food and drink should be used with care, due to their potentially stigmatizing effect, and the potency of the reinforcement. Secondary reinforcement systems like token economies and behavioral contracts should be implemented as appropriate. Reinforcement systems should be inconspicuous enough so as not to draw attention to the inclusion student. Whenever possible, the student should be included in classroom-wide reinforcement systems (token economy, stickers on tests, or extra recess for helping to clean up after lunch). Verbal praise should be used as appropriate within the inclusion setting. An excessive amount of rote or immature sounding verbal praise from a classroom teacher or shadow can easily stigmatize a child within an inclusion setting. Behavior specific verbal praise can be an effective form of reinforcement as well as a strategy to increase student learning. Behavior specific praise reiterates the appropriate behavior that the student is engaging in and links that to praise (i.e. "I like how you shared your toy with Brian," or "Nice sharing, good job!")

C. Data Collection: In order to assess progress (either increase in a skill or decrease in a maladaptive behavior), it is necessary to collect objective data. Without objective data, appropriate decisions regarding program modification cannot be assured. It is largely through objective data collection and analysis that decisions are made regarding modifying the inclusion experience. Data should be reviewed on a regular basis (at least monthly) so that treatment decisions are not delayed. Data collection can involve recording the frequency of a behavior, calculating the percentage of time or intervals where the behavior is observed, recording the duration and severity of a behavior, or in the case of certain instructional programs, trial by trial data. Data may also be collected to determine if a proposed intervention may be socially valid (peer-validity data). In inclusion settings, the data collection process should be as inconspicuous as possible so the classroom environment will not be disrupted or the student stigmatized. Data can be collected by the classroom teacher, shadow or by the student, where appropriate. The data should specifically address areas of weakness that need improvement so that the student may further succeed in inclusion settings. Common target behaviors in inclusion settings include increasing attention to task, independent task completion, sitting appropriately in large groups and increasing spontaneous social interaction with peers. If a student is engaging in a behavior at an intensity requiring large amounts of intrusive data collection, the appropriateness of the inclusion environment for that student should be re-evaluated. Objective data also need to be collected on the student's progress in his/her IEP goals. Goals should be modified only as indicated by objective data analysis. In order to be effective, the consultant, the classroom teacher and the shadow should all agree on effective, necessary and feasible data collection procedures.

D. Behavior Intervention Plans (BIPs): Formal behavior plans are designed to specifically increase an adaptive behavior or decrease a maladaptive behavior. Behavior plans designed for implementation in inclusion settings should be similar in style to those designed for center-based settings. Plans often involve a combination of pro-active strategies (differential reinforcement schedules, environmental modifications, or redirection strategies) and consequence-based strategies (response cost, time out, contingent removal, or additional work assignments). Plans should be individualized for each student. All written intervention plans must include:

1. Clear definitions of the target behaviors to ensure valid assessment and consistency among staff

2. A functional assessment of the behaviors suggesting the underlying function of the behavior for the student

3. A set of antecedent- based strategies to be implemented to prevent the occurrence of the behavior

4. Specific behaviors that may be taught in replacement of the target behavior.

5. Details regarding any procedures to be used as a consequence to a behavior if appropriate (e.g., redirection)

6. Clearly described lists of all of the procedures and strategies to be used with the student

7. Materials needed to carry out the plan

8. Data collection procedures to objectively assess efficacy

9. A schedule of data analysis to inform decision making

10. Schedule of review for the behavior intervention plan

11. Criterion for fading of the plan as well as how it will be faded

12. Criterion for discontinuation of the plan

13. Potential risks if the behavior is untreated

14. Team approval by signature

15. Parental consent by signature

In order for a program to be successful in the development and review of behavior intervention plans, three steps are recommended:

1. Develop a set of Behavior Management/Support Policies and Procedures. These procedures ensure consistency across all staff members.

2. Create a Behavior Management/Support Committee. This committee reviews all BIP's for clinical soundness and the members are well versed and experienced and can provide the person who developed the plan with ideas for alternative options. Plans can be reviewed on a regular schedule that is predetermined dependent on the nature of the plan.

3. Create a Human Rights Committee. This committee's purpose is to review BIP's for ethical concerns related to treatment and human rights. Members of this committee may include some program staff but also community members (e.g., nurse, doctor, psychologists, parent, etc…)

Steps in Formulating a Behavioral Intervention:

1. Based on the information derived from the previous steps, attempt to determine the function of the behavior (as escape, avoidance, tangible, attention-seeking or sensory).

2. Develop a wide array of proactive strategies to try to prevent the behavior from occurring.

3. Identify appropriate alternative behaviors that may serve to replace the maladaptive behavior.

4. Have a reactive plan in place so that for when the behavior does occur, something can be done before the behavior escalates.

Reactive Procedures:

Reactive procedures may already be in place within the classroom for the class in general. Teachers often have reinforcement and punishment procedures set up as a part of their classroom structure. Some examples of these procedures follow.

1. The student loses access to a preferred activity, such as free play or recess.

2. The student loses something contingent upon a behavior (as a happy face sticker).

3. The student sits in a time out chair away from an ongoing activity.

4. The student is separated from other students and is spoken with.

5. The student is removed from the classroom.

Other Reactive Procedures Initiated that may by initiated by the Consultant or Shadow:

1. The student is prompted to stay on-task and work through challenging behavior (e.g., motivation system, gentle reminder, written prompt or schedule).

2. The student is prompted to exhibit appropriate behavior, which is then reinforced.

3. The student who is removed from class must "earn" re-entry. This requires that the classroom be perceived by the student as reinforcing; otherwise, there is little motivation to earn re-entry.

Cautions when Attempting to Treat Maladaptive Behavior:

1. Always treat behavior according to its function; otherwise the intervention may actually make the behavior worse.

2. Know what the reinforcing consequences are in the inclusion environment.

3. Only implement a plan that all involved agree upon.

4. Be realistic and practical: know the limits of the student's classroom. Aside from being willing to implement the plan, the staff must be able to carry it out (follow through).

NOTES:

8. TROUBLESHOOTING

Problems to anticipate and possible solutions:

Professional Partnership Challenges

The successful transition or placement of a student with autism into an inclusion setting involves a partnership among many people at the self-contained, highly structured ABA educational setting and the inclusion site, as well as the student's caretaker(s) or parent(s) to facilitate a successful inclusion experience.

With systematic planning, this partnership has many benefits, including support among professionals, the generation of potential solutions, fewer interruptions in student schedules, shared responsibility, professional and personal growth and development, as well as better and more frequent communication.

In the absence of proactive planning and effective communication, this professional partnership has its challenges, the biggest of which are allotting time to plan, time to meet and coordinating schedules. There may also be limited time and funds available for staff training. The most effective inclusion program includes initial and ongoing staff training and team meetings. In addition, a school/home correspondence system and schedule needs to be developed.

Even if these proactive components are in place at the onset of the inclusion experience, there must be a process for solving problems as they arise. Key components of any effective problem solving effort minimally include:

1. Defining the problem and the desired outcome

2. Troubleshooting ideas for resolution

3. Implementing a plan of resolution that incorporates the best ideas

4. Clarifying who is going to do which parts of the plan and within what timeframe

5. Scheduling a follow up evaluation of the efficacy of the problem solving and resolution

In summary, a successful inclusion program will require the following components prior to student placement:

1. Administrative support – The building principal must understand the needs of the team and know in advance how much time per month the team will need to meet, and whether or not substitute staff need to be available to cover members of the team

2. Planning before the onset of inclusion – During this stage, staff training and consultation schedules should be developed.

3. A formal transition plan that provides details regarding the expected plan including settings, key staff and a timeline for transition. Although the plan may change over the course of the school year it lays a framework for the team to use and provides a structure and expectancy for continuous assessment and monitoring.

4. Parental involvement – The consultant and the building administrator should outline a schedule of parent meetings. Will the parent be invited to attend regularly scheduled team meetings? Should the parent expect daily correspondence? If so, from whom? A home/school communication system should be developed by the team and presented at or before the first team meeting.

5. Clarification of roles and responsibilities – It must be decided in advance who will be responsible for what part of the student's inclusion. Who generates IEP goals? Who implements each? Who provides related services, gym, lunch? Who tracks progress? Who is the "team leader"? To whom does the consultant correspond?

Student Challenges

When transitioning to, and remaining in, an inclusion program, the student will have some areas of success, and some difficulty. As with all other aspects of behavior and learning, it is important to analyze the cause of a student's difficulties in the inclusion setting. Following are the most common causes of problems and recommendations for their correction.

A. Skill deficit:

1. The student didn't learn or have exposure to the skill before going into the inclusion setting.

2. The skill area is a persistent deficit for this student (e.g., abstract language).

3. The student has difficulty getting adult attention in an appropriate way or reacting to delayed response to their needs.

Strategies to be used:

1. *Pre-teaching:* During pre-teaching the student is taught the concept or skill prior to it being taught in the classroom. The shadow or Eden II teacher needs to be aware of specific topics in advance, possibly even using the same curricular materials, so that there will be greater familiarity when the work presented in the classroom.

2. *Post-teaching:* This is a review of the concept, which may continue long after the lesson was presented at the inclusion school, since it may not be reviewed there for a period of time. Materials used may be those used during the lesson, but augmentation with new materials is preferred.

3. *Targeting prerequisite skills:* Provide focused instruction to strengthen foundation skills.

4. *Modification of materials:* By modifying the lesson or materials, the student may be a more active participant during the lesson (e.g., cutting a rectangle in a card to help the student read on the line, or using a pencil with a special grip to help with writing).

5. *Choosing an alternate goal:* Allow the student to use the same materials as the rest of the class but participate on a parallel level (for instance learning about solar system versus making a mobile).

6. *Program for generalization:* When teaching a concept such as big and little or sequencing, use a variety of materials to encourage generalization.

B. Lack of or limited generalization (across people, materials, instructions, or settings)

Strategies to be used:

1. Program for generalization in each area. For example, have the student practice the skill with a number of different people in a few settings and use many different sets of materials.

2. Vary materials and conduct probes. Rather than teaching the student to learn specific responses, teach responses to a limited number of questions within the concept area and probe to see if the student is generalizing beyond those specifically taught. During probe trials, no prompting or reinforcement is given. This shows whether the student is beginning to understand the concept (for example, when targeting the skill of describing items: teach elephant and probe hippopotamus).

C. Perseverative responding/over generalization. Examples of this are giving the same response to all materials or questions and using observational learning of peers when inappropriate.

Strategies to be used:

1. *Promote response variability:* Reinforce any novel responses by the student. This increases the likelihood that the student will use a new response to the same question next time.

2. *Teach discrimination of responses:* Teach responses to other questions so that the student discriminates and responds differently to different questions.

3. *Teach the student when to use observational learning skills:* This is not appropriate during an exam but is appropriate when learning to play a new game. Models can be identified and primed to engage in the desired response while the student with autism is observing.

4. *Use a prompt or cue:* Prompts or cues can be implemented for the student to discriminate and later be systematically faded as student learns this skill.

D. Instruction and materials appear too challenging:

    1. Instruction is unclear to the student.

    2. Instruction is unclear to all students.

    3. Materials are too difficult for student.

Strategies to be used:

    1. *Practice:* Have the student read the instructions again, if written, or present the instructions in written form to help with comprehension. Providing additional practice of a skill at home or at Eden II and providing instructions in a variety of ways are other examples to encourage student mastery.

    2. *Modification of materials:* Slightly modifying a lesson or the materials used may help the student be an active participant during the lesson (e.g., providing a card with a rectangle cut in it to help with reading on the line, or a pencil with a special grip to help with writing) .

    3. *Task analyzing:* By breaking down a difficult task into smaller, more manageable steps, the teacher or shadow may be able to teach the student the beginning steps within a concept, and then the student may learn the rest of the concept in the classroom (e.g., sequencing skills).

    4. *Direction Pairing:* Pair more complex directions with those familiar and known.

    5. *Provide Explanations:* Help teacher understand the array of directions with which the student is already familiar.

E.   Limited attending skills: The student may be capable of learning the lesson but is prevented from doing so by poor attending skills. Possible reasons for poor attending are:

    1. Lack of interest in the lesson, or greater interest in another activity (i.e. self stimulatory behavior)

    2. Particularly difficult time of the day (as after lunch)

3. Anticipation of upcoming or previous activity may be distracting (e.g., gym class is next)

4. Environmental factors may be distracting (as noise level in the room)

5. Lesson may be too long for the student; consider modifications

Strategies to be used:

1. *Provide prompts:* With the provision of a non-intrusive prompt to stay on task, the student may attend to the lesson and actively participate (e.g., gentle reminder).

2. *Increase reinforcement for attending:* By increasing the frequency that reinforcement is provided during that period and by targeting attending behavior it is more likely to increase.

3. *Vary or increase the potency of reinforcers*: Although the aim is to fade reinforcement over time, when a student experiences difficulty in inclusion, more potent reinforcers or a change the criterion for delivery of reinforcement may be necessary.

4. *Increase the student's tolerance to environmental variables and length of lessons:* Develop programs which will increase a student's tolerance, such as waiting, tolerating the word no, and tolerating the termination of an activity.

5. *Teach the student self advocacy:* This will facilitate asking for a break, or planning for a break during extended or challenging lessons.

F. Challenging behaviors

When a behavior persists in inclusion despite the use of motivation systems, curriculum modifications and instructional changes, a functional assessment should be conducted. This assessment may reveal the underlying function of the behavior and point toward relevant interventions.

Steps in Conducting a Functional Behavioral Assessment:

1. Observe, label and define the behavior in the inclusion setting.

2. Complete an "ABC Analysis" by collecting information on the Antecedent, the Behavior and the Consequence. Staff training is necessary regarding how to properly take this type of data.

3. Interview people who are in contact with the student to gather more information about the behavioral issues.

4. Examine environmental events and variables in the setting for any possible relationship.

5. Observe the student in other environments.

6. Determine when, where, and with whom the behavior is **NOT** occurring.

7. Use tools to assist with data collection such as the Motivation Assessment Scale (MAS).

8. Use a variety of data sheets to assist with data collection (e.g., scatterplot, structured ABC)

NOTES:

9. CURRICULAR MODIFICATIONS

Area: Visual Motor Integration

1. Allow the use of "carbonless" paper by another student for note-taking, board copying and assignments.

2. Allow the student to dictate into a voice recorder, or voice-to-text program, and transcribe/print the notes later.

3. Provide extra time for writing down information.

4. Provide photocopied notes.

5. Allow the use of special pencil grip.

6. Put manuscript or cursive alphabet strips on the student's desk.

7. Provide other opportunities to practice writing skills.

8. Allow use of Voice Thread program, if appropriate.

9. If the student is receiving OT/PT services, either direct or through consultation, discuss motor issues with the service provider on a regular basis.

10. Use of Smart Board interactive technology.

Area: Visual Perception

1. Limit the amount of visual stimuli presented at one time.

2. Provide auditory cues when presenting visual information

3. Use color or increased letter size to highlight information

4. Provide visual information in small, manageable amounts

5. Present material through a variety of visual modes, such as books, blackboard, overhead projector, PowerPoint, or interactive technology.

Area: Oral Language/Auditory Processing

1. Present oral directions one step at a time.

2. Paraphrase to simplify information. It may be necessary to teach the student how to respond to teacher directives.

3. Provide visual cues to make verbal instruction more meaningful

4. Establish appropriate attending prior to beginning a lesson or providing oral directions.

5. Allow the student ample time to respond.

6. Repeat directions/questions to give students time to process information.

7. Seat the student near peers who are likely to respond appropriately and in a timely manner to teacher's instructions.

Area: Mathematics

1. Allow the use of a calculator.

2. Use a computer to reinforce and drill skills and facts.

3. Use number lines or tangible representations to explain new skill or concepts.

4. Work from concrete to abstract.

5. Provide ample time to complete task.

6. Develop worksheets that practice foundation skills.

Area: Reading

1. Provide books and texts on audiotape (see appendix for additional resources).

2. Provide supplementary materials the student can read which parallel class work.

3. Give reading material to the student in advance to preview at home or with special service provider.

4. Pre-teach vocabulary.

5. Provide the student with focusing questions or a purpose for reading before reading to help attend to important points.

6. Use a highlighter or card with a hole to stay in place when reading.

7. Teach the student to underline key information.

8. Target phonics systematically to improve word attack skills.

Area: Written Expression

1. Provide student with models of particular formats.

2. Use semantic mapping to organize ideas before writing.

3. Use an electronic speller (see Appendix for resources).

Area: Organizational Skills

1. Provide a student organizer for daily and long term assignments.

2. Establish color coding of assignments, books, notebooks.

3. Establish specific times for homework.

4. Remove distracting stimuli during lesson.

5. Use written and picture prompts for a schedule of the day.

6. Keep all student supplies (such as pencil, scissors and glue) in a specific area such as a box or case.

Area: Test Taking

1. Provide testing modifications as specified on the student's IEP.

2. Provide a study guide or practice questions prior to test.

3. Allow extra time on tests.

4. Provide for a scribe for written tests.

5. Allow the use of a computer for essays or written responses.

6. Provide tests that are typed and enlarged.

7. Provide an alternative testing site.

8. Allow student to respond orally to tests.

9. Allow the student to be tested orally.

10. Provide a reader or scribe during testing sessions.

Area: Note Taking

1. Provide the student with a copy of the teacher's notes before the lesson.

2. Allow the student to tape record the lesson.

3. Provide the student with an outline of the lesson so the student can fill in missing pieces during class.

4. Teach abbreviations, underlining and outlining.

5. Provide prompts to help student take notes at appropriate times.

Area: Homework

1. Provide extra time for the completion of assignments.

2. Provide materials, reading lists and future assignments.

3. Write assignments early in the day to give the student a chance to copy them.

4. Provide feedback on accuracy and adequacy of the student's transcription of homework assignments.

5. Provide a monthly calendar to record long term assignments and projects and their due dates.

6. Attempt to provide some homework assistance to parent(s).

NOTES:

10. POLICIES AND PROCEDURES FOR STAFF WORKING IN INCLUSION SETTINGS

Calendar

The academic calendar can either follow the calendar of the specific school that the student attends or that of the teacher/shadow's employer, if different. The decision about which calendar the student should follow will depend on who is funding his placement and whether the teacher/shadow working with the student is an employee of the school district, a private contractor, or an employee of the student's consultation school. Prior to the student's placement, the specific school calendar the student and teacher/shadow follows should be agreed upon. Depending on the student's placement, it can either be decided at the CSE/CPSE meeting or at a transition meeting within the consultation school/location.

Absence of shadow/teacher

The amount of sick days to which the shadow is entitled is predetermined by the policy of the direct employer. When a shadow is sick he/she must call the direct supervisor, the parent and/or the inclusion school as agreed upon in advance.

Prior to the student starting inclusion, policies on teacher/shadow absence should be established which clarify responsibility for providing a substitute in the case of that eventuality. The team should determine whether the student can remain in school independently or must stay home if a substitute cannot be found.

Absence of Inclusion Site Employees

If the inclusion teacher or shadow is an employee of a school district, sick time and the procedure to follow when the employee is out should proceed according to the district's own policies.

Student Absence

If the student is sick, the student's parent should call the teacher/shadow and school. The teacher/shadow should then call the direct supervisor to inform him/her that the student is sick. Prior to the student beginning in inclusion, the parent should be given a list of contact numbers for notification if the student will be out. A note from the parent, confirming that the student was sick may be required, and must be shared with each site.

Probation

Many employers have a standard probationary period for new employees. During that time the supervisor reserves the right to terminate employment.

Dress Code

When working in an inclusion setting it is important that all individuals dress appropriately and professionally. Business casual is typically acceptable. Dress down items such as mini skirts, shorts and tank tops should not be worn. Shirts bearing inappropriate language and controversial content are not be acceptable attire. The inclusion site may have a dress code that is more or less restrictive than that of the employing organization. If these discrepancies exist, it is best to conform to the code mandating the most professional dress.

Professionalism

An expectation of professional behavior is present at all times. It is important that all staff members understand that they represent their employers and as such act appropriately.

The following issues are critical to remember and perhaps even plan for in order to be prepared to provide appropriate responses:

1. Information regarding students is confidential.

2. Employees may not reveal any information to parents or individuals not directly involved with the student.

3. Questions asked by parents (regarding students other than their own) or members of the community about the student should be deflected or answered without infringing on the rights of the student.

4. If an IEP or progress report is given to a supporting person at the inclusion site, such as a principal, classroom teacher or speech therapist, it should be kept in a locked cabinet or drawer so as not to be accessible to the public.

11. REFERENCES

Baker, J. (2003). Social skills training. Shawnee Mission, Kansas: Autism Asperger Publishing Company.

Bornstein, M. R. Bellack, A. S. & Hersen, M. (1977). Social-skills training for unassertive children: A multiple-baseline analysis. *Journal of Applied Behavior Analysis, 10*, 183-195.

Carr, E. G., Levin, L., McConnachie, G., Carlson, J. I., Kemp, D. C., & Smith, C. (1994). *Communication-Based Intervention for Problem Behavior.* Baltimore: Paul H. Brookes Publishing Co.

Charlop, M. H. (2003). Using video modeling to teach perspective taking to children with autism. *Journal of Positive Behavior Interventions, 5 (1)*, 12-21.

Charlop, M. H. & Milstein, J. P. (1989). Teaching autistic children conversational speech using video modeling. *Journal of Applied Behavior Analysis, 22*, 275-285.

Carr, E. G., & Durand, V. M. (1985). Reducing behavior problems through functional communication training. *Journal of Applied Behavior Analysis, 18*, 111-126.

Cooper, J. O, Heron, T. E., & Heward, W. L. (2007). *Applied Behavior Analysis.* (2nd ed.). New Jersey: Prentice Hall.

Dowrick, P. J. (1991). *Practical Guide to Using Video in the Behavioral Sciences.* USA; John Wiley & Sons, Inc.

Durand, V.M. (1999). Functional communication training using assistive devices: Recruiting natural communities of reinforcement. *Journal of Applied Behavior Analysis, 32*, 247-267.

Eldar, E., Talmor, R., & Wolf-Zukerman, T. (2010). Successes and difficulties in the individual inclusion of children with autism spectrum disorder (ASD) in the eyes of their coordinators. *International Journal of Inclusive Education, 14*, 97-114.

Finke, E. H., McNaughton, D. B., & Drager, K. D. R. (2009). "All children can and should have the opportunity to learn": General education teachers' perspectives on including children with autism spectrum disorder who require AAC. *AAC: Augmentative & Alternative Communication, 25*, 110-122.

Freeman, S., & Dake, L. (1996). *Teach Me Language.* Langley, B.C.: SKF Books.

Friedlander, D. (2009). Sam comes to school: Including students with autism in your classroom. *Clearing House, 82*, 141-144.

Gena, A. (2006). The effects of prompting and social reinforcement on establishing social interactions with peers during the inclusion of four children with autism in preschool. *International Journal of Psychology, 41*, 541-554.

Horrocks, J., White, G., & Roberts, L. (2008). Principals' attitudes regarding inclusion of children with autism in pennsylvania public schools. *Journal of Autism & Developmental Disorders, 38*, 1462-1473.

Johnson, S., Meyer, L. S., & Taylor, B. A. (1996). Supported Inclusion. In C. Maurice, G. Green, & S. Luce (Eds.), Behavioral intervention for young children with autism: A manual for parents and professionals. Austin, Texas: PRO-ED.

Jordan, R. (2008). Autistic spectrum disorders: A challenge and a model for inclusion in education. *British Journal of Special Education, 35*, 11-15.

Krantz, P. J. & McClannahan, L. E. (1993). Teaching children with autism to initiate to peers: Effects of a script-fading procedure. *Journal of Applied Behavior Analysis,. 26*, 121-132.

LeBlanc, L. A. Coates, A. M. Daneshvar, S. Charlop-Christy, M. H. Morris, C. & Lancaster, B. M. (2003). Using video modeling and reinforcement to teach perspective-taking skills to children with autism. *Journal of Applied Behavior Analysis, 36*, 253-257.

Lipsky, D. K., & Gartner, A. (1998). Taking inclusion into the future. *Educational Leadership, 56 (2),* 78-81.

Lynch, S. L., & Irvine, A. N. (2009). Inclusive education and best practice for children with autism spectrum disorder: An integrated approach. *International Journal of Inclusive Education, 13*, 845-859.

Martin, G. & Pear, J. (2006). *Behaviour modification: What is it and how to do it* (8th ed.). Upper Saddle River, NJ: Prentice Hall.

Maurice, C., Green, G. & Luce., S. C. (1996). *Behavioral Intervention for Young Students with Autism.* Austin, Texas: Pro-Ed.

McAFee, J. (2002). Navigating the social world. A curriculum for individuals with asperger's syndrome, high functioning autism and related disorders. Arlington, Texas: Future Horizons.

Neisworth, J. T., & Yingling, B. W. (2002). Videotaped self modeling as a technique for training preschoolers with autism in social-communicative functioning. Pennsylvania State University, 1-28.

Nikopoulos, C.K., & Keenan, M. (2004). Effects of video modeling on social initiations by children with autism. *Journal of Applied Behavior Analysis. 37,* 93-96.

Osborne, A. G., & DiMattia, P. (1994). The IDEA's least restrictive environment mandate: Legal implications, Exceptional Children, 61, 6-14.

Reichle, J. & Wacker, D. P. (1993). *Communicative Alternatives to Challenging Behavior.* Baltimore: Paul H. Brookes Publishing Co.

Schwarz, M. L., & Hawkins, R. P. (1970). Application of delayed reinforcement procedures to the behavior of an elementary school child. *Journal of Applied Behavior Analysis, 3*, 85-96.

Smith Myles, B. & Simpson, R. L. (1998). Asperger Syndrome: A Guide for Educators and Parents. Austin, Texas:Pro-Ed.

Theimann, K. S. & Goldstein, H. (2001). Social stories, written text cues, and video feedback: Effects on social communication of children with autism. *Journal of Applied Behavior Analysis, 34*, 425-446.

Vakil, S., Welton, E., O'Connor, B., & Kline, L. (2009). Inclusion means everyone! the role of the early childhood educator when including young children with autism in the classroom. *Early Childhood Education Journal, 36*, 321-326.

Vitani, T., & Reiter, S. (2007). Inclusion of pupils with autism. *Autism: TheInternational Journal of Research & Practice, 11*, 321-333.

Yianni-Coudurier, C., Darrou, C., Lenoir, P., Verrecchia, B., Assouline, B., Ledesert, B., et al. (2008). What clinical characteristics of children with autism influence their inclusion in regular classrooms? *Journal of Intellectual Disability Research, 52,* 855-863.

NOTES:

Helpful Websites:

A Primer on IDEA:
http://www.cec.sped.org/AM/Template.cfm?Section=Home&CONTENTID
=7839&TEMPLATE=/CM/ContentDisplay.cfm

Overview of No Child Left Behind (NCLB):
http://www2.ed.gov/nclb/overview/intro/4pillars.html

Part 200 regulations for students with Autism Spectrum Disorders:
http://www.p12.nysed.gov/specialed/lawsregs/part200.htm

Overview of FERPA:
http://www2.ed.gov/policy/gen/guid/fpco/ferpa/index.html

Autism Program Quality Indicators:
http://www.vesid.nysed.gov/specialed/autism/apqi.htm

Association for Science in Autism Treatment:
www.asatonline.org

Association for Behavior Analysis International:
http://www.abainternational.org/

Autism Special Interest Group:
http://www.autismpppsig.org/

Council for Disability Rights:
www.disabilityrights.org

Asperger Syndrome Education Network (ASPEN):
http://www.aspennj.org/

National Autism Center:
http://www.nationalautismcenter.org/

Online Asperger Syndrome Information and Support (OASIS):
http://www.aspergersyndrome.org/

Autism Speaks: **Cambridge Center for Behavioral Studies:**
www.autismspeaks.com   http://www.behavior.org/

NOTES:

12. Appendix

A. Peer-Validity Data (to monitor behaviors):
This type of data sheet should be used when a new behavior is identified in an inclusion setting, and the consultant and/or other trained staff are unclear as to whether or not the behavior warrants a formal behavior plan, *when compared to the behavior of peers* in the inclusive setting.

U = Unfocused (blank stares, walking aimlessly, not answering questions)
NCV = Non-Contextual Vocalizations (making animal sounds)

Student: _____   Peer: _____

Time	U	NCV
8:40-8:50		
8:50-9:00		
9:00-9:10		
9:10-9:20		
9:20-9:30		
9:30-9:40		
9:40-9:50		
9:50-10:00		
10:00-10:10		
10:10-10:20		
10:20-10:30		
10:30-10:40		
10:40-10:50		
10:50-11:00		
11:00-11:10		
11:10-11:20		
11:20-11:30		
11:30-11:40		

Time	U	NCV
8:40-8:50		
8:50-9:00		
9:00-9:10		
9:10-9:20		
9:20-9:30		
9:30-9:40		
9:40-9:50		
9:50-10:00		
10:00-10:10		
10:10-10:20		
10:20-10:30		
10:30-10:40		
10:40-10:50		
10:50-11:00		
11:00-11:10		
11:10-11:20		
11:20-11:30		
11:30-11:40		

NOTES:

B. Peer Validity (to monitor attending):

This type of data sheet may be used to determine if the observed student is attending to relevant stimuli (e.g. teacher directions) in the inclusive environment, relative to his/her peers.

Student Name:_____   Date: ___/___/___

Consultant: _____

Activity Title / Description:

_____
_____
_____

Target Student:_____   Peer:_____   total%/#

On Task: ____/___/___/___/___   ___/___/___/___/___   __/__
Direction following:___/___/___/___/___   ___/___/___/___/___   __/__
Respond to adults:___/___/___/___/___   ___/___/___/___/___   __/__
Respond to peers: ___/___/___/___/___   ___/___/___/___/___   __/__
Group responding: ___/___/___/___/___   ___/___/___/___/___   __/__
Initiations to adults:___/___/___/___/___   ___/___/___/___/___   __/__
Initiations to peers:___/___/___/___/___   ___/___/___/___/___   __/__

_____

# of Prompts: ___/___/___/___/___   ___/___/___/___/___   __/__
# of SR: ___/___/___/___/___   ___/___/___/___/___   __/__

NOTES:

C. Inclusion Data Sheet (Skill/Task Oriented):

Student: _____   **Date**: _____

Staff: _____

Time	Activity	# Prompts Curric./Skill	# Prompts Redirect/Att'n	Responses (T)	(P)	Initiations (T)	(P)
12:00							
12:10							
12:20							
12:30							
12:40							
12:50							
1:00							
1:10							
1:20							
1:30							
1:40							
1:50							
2:00							
2:10							
2:20							
2:30							
	Totals:						

Received Reinforcer:

1. _____ YES NO   2. _____ YES NO

3. _____ YES NO   4. _____ YES NO

# Prompts (Curric/Skill)	Tally # of prompts needed to complete work correctly. If there were no prompts needed, put a Ø for that interval.
# Prompts (Redirect)	Tally # of prompts needed to be redirected to activity. If no prompts were needed, put a Ø for that interval.
Responses / Initiations	Tally # of responses / initiations toward teacher (T) and peers (P). Put a P if responses / initiations were prompted.

NOTES:

D. Sample Transition Plan: Transition to Middle School Plan For James Smith

James will be entering The Orlando MS in Sept of 2010. He will require bussing transportation. Times and Routines have yet to be determined. It is important to note that James has consistently demonstrated difficulty controlling his behaviors on a district school bus, in the absence of a matron. "Down" (unstructured) time and reduced amounts of adult supervision are environmental factors that have been determined to contribute to behavior problems.

James will enter all mainstream classes and maintain a regular 6th grade schedule in September. It is not yet known if he will require resource room services for organizational reasons. It is requested by this consultant that guidance plan his schedule accordingly, in the event that James may demonstrate3 the need for additional organizational support.

James typically has difficulty controlling his behavior during unstructured times. During these times, James may be observed to wander about classroom, hallway, bathroom, cafeteria, recess, gym, specials, and auditorium. These behaviors are most frequently observed during the start and end of his day. James is most productive with structured activities and academic based work. He will require very close supervision during these non-structured and transitional times. James has a detailed behavior intervention plan which helps him monitor his own behaviors throughout the school day. Therefore, he will need a full-day 1:1 Shadow. He has benefited from such support in the past.

James's IEP is supported by various home and school services. It is therefore necessary to designate a school coordinator of services. In the past the coordinator of such services was the school psychologist – Dr. M. For the Middle School it is the understanding of this consultant that the responsibility of service coordination will be transferred to Dr. W., who is the Middle School psychologist. Dr. Sgambati (Genesis Autism Consultant) will serve as a laison between school and home personnel as well.

In order to communicate with all members of the IEP team, monthly meetings are recommended. Core staff will include: Parent, 1:1 Shadow, Dr. W., Dr. Sgambati, Speech Language Pathologist, In Home Special Education Teacher, and any other service providers (if relevant). Dr, W. would schedule all these meetings in September for regular intervals over the school year (i.e. the first Friday of every month) and e-mail the schedule to all parties. The meetings should last approximately one period.

E. Sample Transition Goals:

Education:

David will meet with guidance counselor to discuss and assess areas of career interests and postsecondary plans.

By graduation, David will have completed a personal resume and college letter for college admissions.

By graduation, the student will describe his disability in terms of learning strengths and weaknesses.

By graduation, David will attend postsecondary option fairs, events, and sessions provided by the school district.

By graduation, David will participate in traditional standardized tests necessary for acceptance to postsecondary institutions (PSATs, SATs, ACTs, etc).

By graduation, David will research and be prepared to properly apply for financial aide and student loans (i.e. FASA, TAP, etc.).

By graduation, David will tour and meet with education guidance counselors and at four colleges.

By graduation, David will accurately complete three applications to local colleges that offer degrees he is interested in perusing and he is also qualified to attend.

By graduation, David will practice postsecondary education strategies (time management, note-taking techniques, stress reduction techniques, etc) he will need to successfully attend college.

Vocation:
By graduation, student will complete a series of formal and informal vocational assessment techniques (career interest inventories, learning style inventory, student interview, parent interview, etc).

By graduation, David will create a career portfolio and a resume for future employment.

By graduation, student will demonstrate skills necessary to effectively locate, apply, interview, and maintain employment.

By graduation, David will successfully complete a vocational program for the purpose of attaining employable skills to obtain post high school employment.

By graduation, David will volunteer or get part time work in at least 2 different job sites - in the related field of personal interest.

Student will self evaluate work behavior in community-based vocational settings.

Community:

By graduation, David will successfully pass his road test and obtain a driver's license and be able to successfully use public transportation systems (bus, train, taxi, etc).

By graduation, David will be able to budget, save, and handle his own money.

By graduation, David will be able to make and keep all necessary appointments (i.e. interviews, doctors, road test, etc).

By graduation, David will successfully complete all necessary evaluations (i.e. adaptive skill evaluation) in order to apply to OMRDD, Medicaid and SSI.

By graduation, David will be able to successfully access and utilize community resources that could support him after high school.

By graduation, David will know how to be safe in the community and how to get necessary help.

Recreation/Social:

By graduation, David will belong to an appropriate social skill, support group, or interest group.

By graduation, David will be able to call friends, make plans with them, and follow through with plans on a weekly basis.

By graduation, David will identify leisure activities that he can enjoy in his free time.

Independent Living/Domestic Skills:

By graduation, David will be able to plan a daily menu, shop for items, and independently prepare healthy meals.

By graduation, David will be able to accurately clean all rooms of a house or apartment.

By graduation, David will be able to demonstrate appropriate hygiene and self-care (i.e. exercise, well balanced diet, proper sleep routine, and medication management).

By graduation, David will have an appointment with independent living Services to plan for appropriate housing alternatives.

Speech goals:

David will partake in a pragmatic language evaluation, and develop transitional speech goals as per recommendations.

Social/Emotional/Behavioral goals:

David will be able to successfully utilize various coping skills to deal with his anxiety and panic attacks.

David will be able to successfully attend classes on a daily basis.

David will be able to participate in group-activities with peers (i.e. social group, social club, or social gatherings).

F. Consultation Record:

Student: _____   Consultant/Observer: _____
Date: _____   Time: _____

Present during observation:
1. _____
2. _____

I. Follow-up/last observation/team meeting:

    1. _____

    2. _____

II. Behavior observation/Updates:	III. Academic observation/Updates:
_____ _____ _____ _____ _____ _____	_____ _____ _____ _____ _____ _____
IV. Social observation/Updates:	**V. Language/communication:**
_____ _____ _____ _____ _____ _____	_____ _____ _____ _____ _____ _____

VI. Comments/Materials/Resources:

_____
_____
_____
_____

VII. Next observation date: _____ Next meeting date: _____
To be observed next time:

_____

NOTES:

G. SAMPLE Consultation Summary:

Student: MW
Date of Consult: February 5, 2009
In attendance: Dana B (Autism Consultant), Teacher Assistants, students
Class: Periods 5 and 6

Overview:

The focus of today's clinic was to trouble shoot different prompting procedures in order
to improve M's behavior in class. *The recommendations provided below are for M's 1:1 shadow, based on an observation and clinic conducted on 2/5/09.*

Prompting strategies:

At the beginning of class
Prior to entry into the classroom, present M with his progress report, and state the following script:

"Remember, In order to earn a 3, speak with a low volume and do not interrupt." (Present this information in a neutral tone). If M interrupts, maintain a neutral tone, and repeat the statement again. Once he is quiet, allow him to transition into class. Once seated, maintain close proximity to M, and state the following script: "If you do you work independently, then you can have space while in class."

During class time
Provide written verbal praise with positive statements approximately every 10 minutes (i.e. "great job M!" Samples have been provided during probe sessions and relayed to 1:1 shadow on 2/5/09.

When M is on task, fade your proximity in intervals of 3 feet (i.e. if he is reading with the group, move back 3 feet. If he continues to remain on task, move back another three feet, so you are a total of 6 feet away).

At the end of the period (between classes)
If M meets his contract, review with him the specific areas that he excelled in (i.e. followed teacher directions, kept his voice low, etc).

Summary:

Overall, we need to continue to model and facilitate positive interactions between M and peers and adults. When M is non-compliant, remind him of how he can earn a "3" on his progress report. NOTE: he should be reminded of his progress report prior to every period, so that he is not only discussing his progress report when he is engaged in noncompliant behavior.

Dana B
Clinical Coordinator of Outreach Services

H. Prompting Graph:

This graph is to be used to monitor the number of prompts provided to a student during a given activity. Two specific examples for use of a prompting graph are for peer validity (i.e., graphing the number of prompts needed for the student in question versus his/her peer), and/or generalization of stimulus control (i.e., the number of prompts provided by a classroom teacher versus a 1:1 shadow).

Student Name: _____   Program: _____
                                          Year: _____

20	
18	
16	
14	
12	
10	
8	
6	
4	
2	
0	
Month	
Day	

NOTES:

I. INCLUSION READINESS CHECKLIST

(Note that PREREQUISITE skills are identified in purple and BENEFICIAL skills are identified in blue).

Criteria and readiness skills ages 3-6 (school setting)

Child's Name: _____   Age: _____

Evaluator(s): _____   Date of Evaluation: _____

Note whether the student has the skills, the skill is emerging, or the skill was not observed:

Prerequisite for LRE	Has Skill	Emerging	Not Observed	Comments
Remains on task for at least 5 minutes				
Responds to delayed contingencies (tokens)				
Responds to delayed contingencies (behavior contract)				
Responds to name				
Waits for teacher's attention (at least 1 minute)				
Waits quietly for an activity to begin (at least 2 minutes)				
Initiates at least 5 phrases/comments				
Initiates at least 5 questions				

Prerequisite for LRE	Has Skill	Emerging	Not Observed	Comments
Toilet trained and can initiate for the bathroom				
Sits appropriately in a group (at least 7-10 minutes)				
Sits quietly in a group (at least 5 minutes)				
Sits appropriately in a group (at least 7-10 minutes)				
Sits quietly in a group (at least 5 minutes)				
Sits quietly in a group (at least 5 minutes)				
Follows one step directions with teacher at least 6-8 feet away				
Responds to simple questions from teacher				
Maladaptive behavior < 30%				

Prerequisite for LRE	Has Skill	Emerging	Not Observed	Comments
Can tolerate noise and commotion of a typical classroom				
Can tolerate termination of an activity before completion				
Can transition to and from various activities appropriately				
Can identify colors receptively and expressively				
Can identify shapes receptively and expressively				
Can identify letters receptively and expressively				
Can identify numbers receptively and expressively				

Note whether the student has the skills, the skill is emerging, or the skill was not observed:

BENEFICIAL for LRE	Has Skill	Emerging	Not Observed	Comments
Can tolerate sitting/playing within 1-2 inches of a peer				
Initiates greetings to peers				
Initiates greetings to teachers				
Reciprocates greetings with teachers				
Reciprocates greetings with peers				
Initiates at least 5 simple questions/comments to peers				
Initiates at least 5 simple questions to peers				
Responds to simple questions from peers				

BENEFICIAL for LRE	Has Skill	Emerging	Not Observed	Comments
Reciprocates conversational statements with peers				
Can play with a toy independently				
Can share with peers				
Can take turns with a peer				
Can line up and remain in line with peers				
Gains teacher's attention when needed				
Can ask for help				
Can direct eye contact toward peer/adult				
Can direct eye contact toward object/activity				

Criteria and readiness skills ages 7-10 (school setting)

Child's Name: _____ Age: _____

Evaluator(s): _____ Date of Evaluation: _____

Note whether the student has the skills, the skill is emerging, or the skill was not observed:

Prerequisite for LRE	Has Skill	Emerging	Not Observed	Comments
Can identify the letters in the alphabet				
Can sound out all letters in the alphabet				
Can identify numbers and count				
Can write the alphabet				
Can write his/her name				
Can match identical pictures				
Can match non-identical pictures				
Can identify 50 familiar objects				
Has computer skills				
Can retrieve books/materials/supplies				

Prerequisite for LRE	Has Skill	Emerging	Not Observed	Comments
Can answer concrete calendar questions				
Can read 3-4 word sentence				
Can read silently				
Can follow worksheets top/bottom/left/right				
Can comprehend "WH" questions				
Can identify cause and effect				
Can recall past events				
Can color/paste simple art activities				

Prerequisite for LRE	Has Skill	Emerging	Not Observed	Comments
Can follow 2-3 step directions				
Can sit quietly/appropriately for 20-30 minutes				
Can raise his/her hand				
Has group responding skills				
Can tolerate noise and commotion of a typical classroom				
Can transition to and from various activities				
Can stay on task for 10-20 minutes				
Will wait up to 5 minutes appropriately				

Beneficial for LRE	Has Skill	Emerging	Not Observed	Comments
Discriminates when to raise hand and when not to				
Will answer name, age, phone number, address, birthday				
Reciprocates information				
Can run/jump/catch ball				
Initiates for help				
Raises hand to seek assistance				
Expresses needs (verbally and nonverbally)				
Requests items from peer without grabbing				

Beneficial for LRE	Has Skill	Emerging	Not Observed	Comments
Takes turns with peers				
Models peer activities				
Follows classroom rules				
Can learn skills observational learning				
Can learn new information in a large group setting				
Raises hand during group instructions				
Understands safety issues such as: not leaving building/fire drill/calling for help				
Initiates at least 5 simple questions/comments to peers				

Beneficial for LRE	Has Skill	Emerging	Not Observed	Comments
Initiates at least 5 simple questions/comments to peers				
Initiates at least 5 simple questions/comments to teachers				
Initiates for the bathroom				
Independently uses the bathroom (pull up pants/wipe, etc.)				
Takes care of personal hygiene – wash hands				
Can button				
Can use zipper				
Can snap				

NOTES:

J. ABC Data Sheet: Antecedent – Behavior – Consequence (ABC) data collection

Complete this form when instances of behaviors are observed.

Student: _____

Date	Staff	Time	Antecedent	Behavior	Consequence

NOTES:

Made in the USA
Lexington, KY
28 January 2013